THE
MUNCEY MUSIC
BOOK

ANTHONY TWINER

DANCE BOOKS
Cecil Court, London

First published in 1986 by Dance Books Ltd.,
9 Cecil Court, London WC2N 4EZ.

ISBN 0 903102 92 7

Designed by Tina Dutton
Production in association with
Book Production Consultants, Cambridge.
Typeset by Goodfellow & Egan, Cambridge.

THE
MUNCEY MUSIC
BOOK

INTRODUCTION

Richard Muncey was an exceptionally talented musician, and his untimely death robbed the profession of a pianist who could improvise in any style that was required, as well as sight-read a piece of music correctly in tempo and quality, with an accuracy that many a professional would envy.

I had the pleasure of working with Richard for over twenty years, and learnt much from him about the practical application of music to movement. Moreover, he endeared himself to everyone by his sense of humour, his interest in one's work, and not least by the fact that he would arrive punctually for any engagement, always carrying his umbrella, whatever the weather!

One of his major interests was extending the musical knowledge of the teachers and students he played for. This short book is an attempt to carry on his good work in presenting the basics of music to those who study dance in all its different aspects and styles. Throughout his career he maintained that music was the basis of dance; and when correctly played and of good quality, then the teacher, student and performer would respond. Frequently he was faced with the problem of music badly cut, used at the wrong tempo, etc., and he felt that music, its study and appreciation should be more of an integral part of a dancer's training and not just subservient to the technique of movement.

In the various publications of Robert Harrold and myself on national character dancing, he not only edited the music of the traditional dances, but composed the piano pieces for the choreographic solos; and in every case created works that reflected the instruments and harmony of the music of the chosen country or region.

He also played for our annual teachers' courses and gave invaluable help and advice to many in the dancing profession. Much of his playing has been recorded on tape which is invaluable.

When the London College of Dance and Drama was situated in Marylebone Lane, Anita Heyworth appointed him to the staff, where he gave instruction and help to the students. Because of his facility in accompanying so many styles of dance, he often played for the examinations in the Ballet, Modern, National and Greek branches of the Imperial Society of Teachers of Dancing.

This book, written by Anthony Twiner, first pianist and conductor of the Royal Ballet, is a memorial to someone sadly missed by so many in the dancing profession.

Helen Wingrave

THE
MUNCEY MUSIC
BOOK

DANCER – Considering that music is probably the prime inspiration of ballet and the dance, I have always felt concerned that we dancers are so ill informed about the subject. Music books are usually written for practising musicians and are therefore rather loaded with technicalities and specialised language, a lot of which is beyond the understanding of many people who do not play a musical instrument. I was therefore wondering whether it would be possible to have the basic facts about music explained in simple language so that dancers could understand more about the music they either have to dance to, or which they need to use for choreography.

MUSICIAN – I think I understand what you mean by music being the prime inspiration of ballet, but to put it a little more correctly, the ideas and stories for ballet are obviously derived from literary sources, or from the very imaginative mind of a choreographer, whereas the inspiration for the actual choreography comes of course from the music chosen, or commissioned, by the choreographer. I have always felt that music is a subject much neglected in the curriculum of ballet schools and indeed in education in general. Even when *I* was at school, and that isn't too long ago, each class used to receive musical training two or three times a week; that mainly consisted of learning to read a melodic line to enable one to sing a tune reasonably well at sight, in other words to be able to understand signs relating to rhythm and pitch. Also, we learnt how to beat time like a conductor – perhaps that was what sowed the seeds of ambition in my mind!

It would greatly help a dancer, I believe, to learn these things, as I have lost count how many times a soloist has asked me just before a performance, 'What do you do before my variation?' – meaning what preparatory beat do I give before the music starts! Such very basic knowledge as this is sadly lacking in both students and professionals, I fear. It would therefore please me a great deal to do as you suggest and try to explain a few of the mysteries of music in simple language! However, I would like first to talk about music generally in relation to the dance.

I must admit that I smile when I hear people talk about 'musical' dancers – what do they really mean by that expression, I wonder? Perhaps it might surprise you to learn that there are even unmusical musicians! There are, of course, hosts of performers with brilliant and amazing techniques, but when they play they leave one feeling cold and unsatisfied due to the fact that their interpretative powers and expressive abilities are undeveloped. You see, I believe that phrasing is the very essence of all music. If you had to listen to a speech or lecture by someone who spoke on a monotone or at the same pitch the whole time, you would soon be bored, and whatever message the speaker was trying to convey would be utterly lost to you. If you listened to a pianist playing just the notes of a piece without any expression, you would, I hope, be similarly unimpressed. Unfortunately one hears many ballet studio pianists who play in this way, perhaps as a result of the repetitive nature of their work, but it reflects a great deal on the students, I fear.

An important aspect of phrasing is **emphasis**. One hears musicians who, when playing a passage marked forte, or loud, give equal emphasis to each note in that passage. This is really ridiculous!

When we speak, we do not give equal emphasis to every syllable – why should we do so when singing or playing music, or indeed dancing? I can shout at you, but some syllables will still be uttered relatively quietly, still giving a sense of rise and fall in the voice. A musical and intelligent dancer should be able to convey in her performance that sense of shape or curve, by giving some steps more stress or importance than others, and this often involves the element of speed. One often hears a dancer being instructed to 'get on the beat'. That is all very well as a general rule, but how boring it is when every beat is accorded its own particular step! What is important is how a dancer moves 'within' a phrase. Therefore, how much better it would be if she were advised to 'listen to the phrase', and so respond to the rise and fall of the notes, or to the different accents or highlights within that phrase.

In my early days as a dance accompanist, I used to look forward to that section in an exam called 'musical interpretation', when a candidate was asked to listen to a short piece of music and then react to it in movements appropriate to the mood. This reaction to music is a necessary part of being musical, I think. A ballet dancer has to react in many ways in a performance – to a change of tempo perhaps, or when a solo instrument in the orchestra fails to come in on cue! I once asked a ballerina, after a performance of *Swan Lake*, what she thought of the solo violin playing that evening. Her jaw dropped, and she stuttered out 'I can't really say, I wasn't listening'. To give her the benefit of the doubt, she *was* listening of course, but to the basic melody and the tempo that the violinist was playing, rather than the *quality* of the sound produced.

It is a fact of life nowadays that there is so much background music wherever one goes, in shops, hotels, transport, films and television and not least the home, that people have got into the habit of merely hearing music and not listening to it. At the next performance, I suggested that she tried hard to listen and then comment on the quality of the music she was dancing to, not merely the aspects of it which immediately concerned her. I am glad to report that she has since become quite an astute critic!

DANCER – Well, listening to music obviously forms a very important part of a dancer's life, but I suppose music is something akin to a foreign language, in that although one can appreciate it and understand it aurally, it means much more and offers wider opportunities if one can actually read it as well. But the trouble is that music books are written for students of music and therefore are a little beyond the understanding of non-performers.

MUSICIAN – Yes, I think it is a tremendous advantage for a dancer, and especially a teacher or choreographer, to read music, even if it means to understand only the very basics of the notation. There are many famous choreographers who cannot read music and who rely solely on the musician to explain it to them. Thank goodness that choreologists, who notate the dance movements, are also taught the basics of music notation to help them relate the steps to the correct passage in the music.

I should very much like to try and explain simply the very basic facts of musical notation, and I think that as a dancer would, on the whole, need only to read a piano score and not a complicated orchestral layout, I will confine my exposition within the framework of a piano score.

When I have been playing rehearsals, dancers have often come and peered over my shoulder, frowning hard and trying to gain some enlightenment from the hieroglyphics on the printed page! And if one is attempting to do some choreography, however simple, it surely must be a help to understand how and why the music is written in the way it is. Before we consider how music is notated, let us just think about 'sound' itself. Sound is of course anything that we can hear: the noise of traffic, a dog barking, the wind in the trees, or a bird singing in the garden. When a human voice sings, it can carry further than a speaking voice. Have you noticed how, when we call people from a distance, we often raise our voices higher than in normal conversation, and the words are given an actual pitch? In music any definite sustained level of sound is a **note** and the height or depth of any note is its **pitch**. The physical origin of a note is vibration, and it is the regular vibrations that produce musical sounds. Most of us have access to a piano, and to explain the meaning of musical notes it would be helpful to look at a keyboard, because there, unlike on a stringed or woodwind instrument, one can actually see all the notes all the time. Most music is based on merely seven notes, with five extra notes to be used when required. The seven notes are given the same names as the first seven letters of the alphabet A – G, and these happen to be the white notes on a piano, the black ones being the five extra notes grouped in twos and threes in a pattern between the white notes, and this pattern recurs regularly over and over again along the whole length of the keyboard. But for our purpose, it would be best to look at the group of notes in the middle of the instrument where the note C is called middle C.

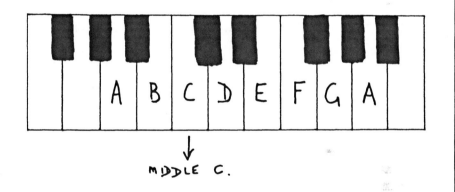

MIDDLE C.

The seven main notes, when they are heard one after another, are like the rungs of a ladder, and musicians call that ladder a **scale**. However, the ladder is incomplete without the eighth rung which is called the **octave**. This is not really a new note, it is A again, but instead of being at the bottom, it is now at the top of the completed ladder, and it in turn can be the bottom note of a new scale. The steps in the scale are not all spaced at the same distance soundwise. The space between B and C, and between E and F, is only half the size of the other steps, and that is because there is no black note between them. Whole steps are called **tones**, half-sized steps are **semitones**, and the difference in sound between these two are of paramount importance in music, especially where intervals are being considered, but before I talk about intervals we must first learn about music notation.

The writing of musical notation is a fascinating story of evolution and a subject really beyond the scope of this little book. Suffice it to say that, about a thousand years ago, melodies were written on, above and below a single horizontal line. Later on three more lines were added giving greater scope for more elaborate tunes, and later still a fifth line appeared, and these five lines are called a **stave**. Let us look at what appears at the beginning of a piece of piano music. Normally piano music is written on two staves, one for each of our two hands, but joined together by a vertical line and a more ornate brace.

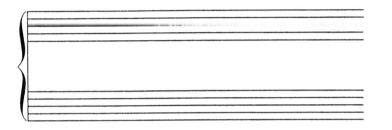

Each stave has a sign at the beginning to denote whether the pitch is above or below middle C, and this sign, which is an elaborate version of either the letter G or F, is called a **clef**, because in early days it was a key, or clue to knowing the pitch of an individual horizontal line. The G clef is now known as the **treble clef**, and the F clef is called the **bass clef**. If we imagine another horizontal line between the two staves, that line would represent the note middle C,

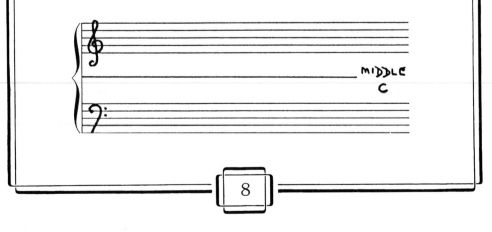

but for all notes that are too high or too low for the stave, we use short lines parallel to the stave, and these are called **leger lines**.

DANCER – But surely the spaces between the lines are also used?

MUSICIAN – Yes, indeed they are, and if we look at how a scale is written on a stave, we can see clearly how both the lines and spaces are used alternately.

DANCER – Why did you choose those particular notes?

MUSICIAN – For a very good reason. One thing concerning music most of us learn at school is tonic sol-fah, that is, doh, ray, me, fah, soh, lah, te, doh. Why, even in that marvellous musical *The Sound of Music*, one of the most memorable numbers deals with that very subject! If I were to ask you to sing those eight notes they would sound exactly like the notes I used in the above example, which on the piano are all white notes. If you were to play eight consecutive white notes beginning on any note other than C, they would sound wrong, because the spacing of tones and semitones would be different. The tonic sol-fah system will help us later too, when we deal with intervals and the meaning of major and minor keys. Oh, and by the way, you will have noticed that all notes are written in small circles, but in earlier days notes were square, because at that time quill pens were used.

So, to recap, we have two staves, each of which has a clef sign telling us which note is represented on which line. There are two other signs to be seen at the beginning of a piece – namely a **key-sign** or signature and a **time-signature**.

For a non-performer the key-sign is relatively unimportant, and I do not feel I should say much about it on this occasion – remember I am trying to deal with only the very basic facts which will help a dancer to understand music.

To a musician the key in which a piece is written is of vital importance, and is represented by signs which we call **sharps**, **flats** and **naturals**, but I do not want you to concern yourself about these.

What is much more important to you as a dancer, is the second sign denoting the time-signature, but even before that can mean anything to you, we must learn about the different values of the written notes, which themselves represent **rhythm**.

This sign **o** is called a semibreve, but a better name for it is the American expression 'whole-note.'

This sign ♩ is called a minim, but in America – a half-note.

These are the only 'white' musical signs. The remainder are all black!

This sign ♩ represents a crotchet or quarter-note.

This sign ♪ is a quaver or an eighth-note.

And so it continues!

All these notes have a relationship to the first one mentioned, the semibreve or whole-note, and each one is half the value of its predecessor. To help us understand this re-lationship, it would perhaps be a good idea to write down these note-values as they relate to a well-known nursery rhyme.

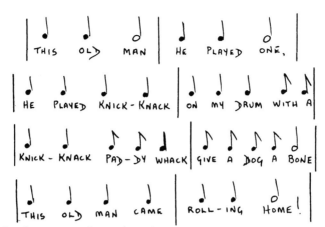

The single vertical strokes between the several notes are called **bar-lines**, and the distance in time from one bar-line to the next is a **bar** though Americans call it a **measure**. So now we can learn and understand our first time-signature, $\frac{4}{4}$. A time-signature looks like a fraction because it has two numbers, the one underneath telling us what the unit of time is (and this is where the American expressions are of great help) in this case a quarter-note, or crotchet. The number above tells us how many units the bar contains, in this example also four. I am sure we all know the tune of *Knick-Knack Paddy Whack*, so perhaps we might look at it as written on a stave, and if you have a piano within reach, you could even pick out the notes to play yourself!

$\frac{4}{4}$ is sometimes referred to as **march time** or even **common time**. You may find in some editions of music that instead of $\frac{4}{4}$ the time signature is represented by a C. Contrary to popular belief, it is not a symbol for the word 'common' – it is just a relic from the medieval system of notation, and is meant to be a half-circle. One often sees also the C with a vertical stroke through it – ₵ . This is known by musicians as **alla breve**, an archaic and far from helpful expression, but meaning that there should be a feeling of two main beats in the bar, rather than four, or to be more specific $\frac{2}{2}$!

The $\frac{3}{4}$ time-signature is understood by many to be principally that of waltz-time, but it is vitally important for a dancer, especially a teacher, to know that it is also the time-signature of two other common dance forms – those of the mazurka and the polonaise. But I should prefer to go into that more deeply a little later on!

We need now to consider dotted notes. Whatever the time-signature may be, a dot after any note always makes it half as long again. See how this makes sense when you look at the rhythm of *God Save the Queen*.

In particular, to make the last note equal three crotchets we have to dot the minim, (a minim is equal to two crotchets, remember, therefore a dotted minim lasts for three crotchets).

So, we have learned that when a crotchet is the unit of time in a piece of music, it is represented by the lower figure 4, as in $\frac{2}{4}$ $\frac{3}{4}$ $\frac{4}{4}$. In the same way, a quaver, or eighth-note, can be the unit of time and is represented by the figure 8 in a time-signature: $\frac{3}{8}$ $\frac{4}{8}$ $\frac{6}{8}$ $\frac{9}{8}$ etc. $\frac{3}{8}$ is the time-signature for music with three quavers to the bar, but the beat itself need be no quicker than the beat in a $\frac{3}{4}$ time. The speed will depend on the indication at the beginning of the piece, and we will consider these terms relating to speed a little later on. I well remember the occasion when a dance teacher asked me to play a $\frac{3}{8}$ for a particular exercise in class. She indicated no speed and was somewhat dismayed by the blank look I gave her! This is the danger of using terms which one does not really understand – all she needed to say was 'a slow or a quick three'.

Remember, the unit of time gives no indication whatsoever of speed. A tune in $\frac{4}{8}$ with four quavers to the bar, is like one in $\frac{2}{4}$ with two crotchets to the bar, except that it would be counted in quavers.

Now we come to what can be rather a confusing time-signature $\frac{6}{8}$. There are six quavers to the bar here, but *not* three groups of two, but two groups of three!

The six quavers to the bar in the above example are counted **123456**, and not as in a bar of $\frac{3}{4}$ – **123456** or '1 and 2 and 3 and'. However, not many $\frac{6}{8}$ tunes are slow enough to be counted in six, but are counted with a dotted crotchet beat, i.e. two main beats to the bar, each beat having three quavers to it. What a mouthful, but fairly easy to understand, I hope!

A $\frac{9}{8}$ bar is like three bars of $\frac{3}{8}$ joined together and usually counted in three dotted crotchet beats to the bar.

A $\frac{12}{8}$ bar is like four bars of $\frac{3}{8}$ or two bars of $\frac{6}{8}$ joined together and counted in four dotted crotchet beats to the bar.

Time-signatures with a dotted-note beat are called **compound**, whereas those with a whole note beat are called **simple**. In simple time, the beat is divided into two, whereas in compound time the beat is divided into three.

To summarise then:

$\frac{2}{2}$ $\frac{2}{4}$ $\frac{2}{8}$ are **simple duple** time-signatures.

$\frac{3}{2}$ $\frac{3}{4}$ $\frac{3}{8}$ are **simple triple** time-signatures.

$\frac{4}{2}$ $\frac{4}{4}$ $\frac{4}{8}$ are **simple quadruple** time-signatures.

$\frac{6}{4}$ $\frac{6}{8}$ $\frac{6}{16}$ are **compound duple** time-signatures (where the unit of time would be a $\frac{1}{16}$ note or a semiquaver.

$$\frac{9}{4} \quad \frac{9}{8} \quad \frac{9}{16}$$ are **compound triple** time-signatures.

$$\frac{12}{4} \quad \frac{12}{8} \quad \frac{12}{16}$$ are **compound quadruple** time-signatures.

I must not forget to mention that there are several time-signatures that do not belong to the above categories. These include **quintuple**, where there are five beats to the bar, but which can be felt as 2+3 or 3+2. Think of the second movement of Tchaikovsky's sixth symphony as an example.

Then there are **septuple** time-signatures, where the bar can often be counted as 3+4 or 4+3. Many Balkan folk melodies have seven beats to a bar.

Before we leave note-values and time-signatures, and especially after illustrating the difference between simple and compound times, I must mention the importance of twelfth-notes or triplet quavers in Jazz dance and Tap. These are simply quarter-notes or crotchets, subdivided into three equal eighth-notes. You will see what this means, I hope, when you look at the following example, which consists of the first two phrases of that well known song from *The King and I* – '*Getting to know you*'!

All the signs that I have explained so far relate to the sounds we hear, but there are of necessity signs which denote periods of silence, or as we call them, **rests**.

Now that we have learnt to recognise all the note values, all we need to do is to learn the corresponding rests. These are as follows:

Semibreve or whole-note rest

UNDER A LINE.

Minim or half-note rest

ON A LINE.

Crotchet or quarter-note rest

OR

IN SOME EDITIONS

Quaver or eighth-note rest

Semiquaver or sixteenth-note rest

DANCER – Well, I feel that I ought to stop you here because I consider that what you have explained so far amounts to the very basic knowledge that a dancer needs to be able to read music sufficiently. Any further information would be beyond my understanding at the moment and in any case, were I to need any more advanced knowledge, there are many text books to which I could refer.

MUSICIAN – Yes, perhaps you are right. If you have been able to take in the preceding information, you can at least now look at a piano score, see the time-signature and be able to decipher the rhythm of a melody and indeed to see how it rises and falls in pitch. But, there are a number of other things which help us to understand how a piece of music sounds, for example the indications as to speed, quality and dynamics.

Let's deal with 'speed' first. I think this presents the dancer or choreographer with the biggest problems of all. More mistakes are made in this area than in all others put together I feel, especially where choreography is concerned. Whether you wish to make up a two-minute solo for a young pupil, or, at the other extreme, a complete ballet, if you are unsure as to the speed a composer intended for his music, seek advice from a musician before you set one step! There are still, alas, many such errors made by even very reputable choreographers. I always remember working with Nureyev on his production of the *Nutcracker* and feeling very uneasy, to say the least, about the tempi that he had adopted for his choreography. When the conductor realised what he was going to have to do, he was so upset that I think he insisted that a note be put in the programme blaming Nureyev for all the slow tempi!

Having said that, I firmly believe that there is a reasonable limit either side of a given tempo marking, but it is when that limit is abused that the situation becomes unacceptable. A composer always places some indication of speed at the beginning of his work, sometimes adding what we call a 'metronome mark' to tell us exactly how many beats there should be within one minute. For example, ♩ = 60 shows that it would take a minute for 60 crotchets to be sung or played, and a second hand of a watch can always be used for timing this and any related speeds. But the main instructions as to speed are usually given in Italian terms, although French and German composers often use their own languages for this purpose. Perhaps a list of the more common Italian terms would be useful, and I will start with the slow speeds and get progressively quicker though

I will keep to three main categories: slow, moderate and fast.

largo
lento   **slow**
adagio

andante
moderato   **moderate**
allegretto

allegro
vivace
presto   **fast**
prestissimo

There are a few other terms related to tempo that are very important to us, mainly rallentando (rall.), ritardando or ritenuto (rit.) and accelerando (accel.).

Music often slows down before coming to rest, and this is indicated by either the word rallentando or ritardando. Ritenuto implies really a holding back of the tempo, or indeed a sudden slower tempo altogether. An alternative expression that is seen quite often is 'meno mosso', literally, less movement. Of course, these are not used only at the end of the piece but can appear at any time where there is a relaxation of speed required. On the other hand, if the pulse in the music is to become gradually quicker, then the word accelerando is used, but if a sudden quicker tempo is required then it is more usual to see the words 'piu mosso', literally more movement. After either of these changes of speed, 'a tempo' or 'tempo primo' is written to denote a return to the original speed.

DANCER – You said you were going to talk about expression marks and dynamics, but do you think these are so very important to a dancer's knowledge of music?

MUSICIAN – Yes indeed I do. As I stated earlier, music does not consist merely of notes – it is the way in which these notes are related and joined together, or phrased, that is important to us, and that can affect our understanding of the quality of music. I think we all know, for example, what a tarantella is – an energetic Italian dance, usually in a quick $\frac{6}{8}$ time and virtually all the notes, both of the melody and accompaniment, should be played in a detached way, or as a musician would say, staccato. I always imagine that the piano keys are very hot and must be released as soon as possible! But if it were played in a very smooth manner or legato, the whole character of the music would be changed and it would not inspire you to dance those quick crisp steps in the proper manner. I have also heard pianists who, although playing staccato with their fingers, ruin the whole effect by holding down the sustaining pedal with their right foot!

It is therefore important to have some knowledge of the terms relating to the way a piece of music is to be played, as well as those pertaining to speed. I have already mentioned staccato, meaning detached or separated, but sometimes it is shown merely by placing a dot above or below the note, e.g. ♩ ♩ . Do not confuse those with the notes that are lengthened in value by having dots placed *after* them! At the beginning of a tarantella, a composer might write 'sempre staccato', meaning that all the notes in the entire piece should be played in a detached manner.

The opposite of staccato is legato, meaning smooth. This is often indicated by curved lines or slurs over the notes to show the phrasing.

Other widely used words for expression, or mood, are: espressivo (expressive), dolce (sweetly), sostenuto (sustained), animato (lively), leggiero (lightly).

Dynamics is the word we use to refer to the different degrees of loudness in music. The two most common are forte, written *f*, meaning loud, and piano (*p*) meaning soft or quiet. Other terms relating to dynamics are:

fortissimo	*ff*	very loud
pianissimo	*pp*	very soft
mezzo forte	*mf*	moderately loud
mezzo piano	*mp*	half way between mezzo forte and piano

Growing louder is crescendo (cresc.) or $<$

Growing softer is diminuendo (dim.) or $>$

DANCER – Yes, I can see now that expression and dynamics are most important in our appreciation of music, and I can understand how the ballerina you mentioned earlier was eventually inspired more by the quality of the music than by being merely concerned with its tempo. Now, there is one term in musical theory that you have not yet discussed in detail, one which appears quite often when we have to consider the music for national or character dances, and that is **intervals**.

MUSICIAN – Indeed, that word can present problems! I remember playing for the national exam once, when one candidate was actually asked what an interval was. She thought hard for a few seconds and then replied: 'It means a pause'. Well, there is some sort of logic in that guess, but it is not the correct answer! It is actually quite a complicated subject for a non-musician but I will try to explain the basic ideas behind it as simply as I can.

An 'interval' is the relationship between two given notes, and more specifically, the distance in pitch between those two notes. I explained earlier about scales and tonic sol-fa – these can be of great help to us in our understanding of intervals.

We don't even need to play an instrument to get to grips with the simpler intervals, provided we can sing a scale in tonic sol-fah, and I am sure most of us can do that! However, for clarity's sake, we can look at a scale made up of the white notes on a piano where doh is the note C.

Intervals are always measured from the lower note to the upper, never the other way about. First of all, let us think about the relationship between doh and each ascending note in turn. If we call doh note number 1, and ray number 2, we call the interval between these two notes a **second**.

Similarly,
between doh(1) and me(3), the interval is called a **third**
between doh(1) and fah(4), the interval is called a **fourth**
between doh(1) and soh(5), the interval is called a **fifth**
between doh(1) and lah(6), the interval is called a **sixth**
between doh(1) and te(7), the interval is called a **seventh**
between doh(1) and doh(8), the interval is called an **octave**.

However, if we wanted to measure the interval between say ray(2) and soh(5), we should have to consider the note ray as if it were doh! It would be of no use subtracting two from five and saying the interval was a third, because as you will see when it is written on the stave, the interval between these two notes is in fact a fourth!

Now another complication! I am sure you will have heard mentioned with regard to music from Eastern Europe and the Balkans, the interval of an augmented second. This is not easy for some people to understand but I will try to shed some light on it! If you can look at a keyboard while reading the next section, it could make things easier for you, but in any case I will show a diagram of that part of the keyboard with which we are concerned.

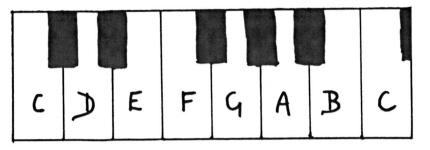

So far, we have only needed to look at the white notes on the piano, but now we must consider the black notes, which are the five extras placed between certain of the white notes. Their pattern of twos and threes recurs again and again over the whole keyboard, of course. Before we can proceed further, I want to enlarge upon what I said earlier about tones and semitones. Look first at the diagram below.

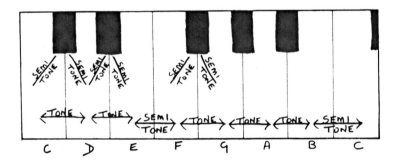

You can see that the distances in sound between most adjacent white notes is a tone, but between E and F, and B and C, the distance is only half a tone (or a semitone), because there is no black note between them. If we play consecutively all the notes between lower C and upper C, including the black notes, we will have played a **chromatic** scale, i.e. a scale consisting entirely of semitones. Now we have already learned, I hope, that the interval between C (doh) and D (ray) is a second. Look at the black note between notes D and E (me). That black note can be called one of two things; either D sharp 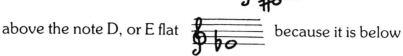 because it is

above the note D, or E flat because it is below

E. It sounds the same of course when we play it alone, but it is its relationship with other notes that determines whether it is called D sharp or E flat. So the interval between the written note C and D sharp is called an augmented second because it has been enlarged by a semitone. The interval between the written notes C and E flat is called not, as you might expect by assuming the opposite, a diminished third, but in this case a minor third. We have not really thought about the words major and minor in this discussion, and to explain it properly I would prefer to be able to actually play to you, but try it for yourself. Play slowly the notes, C, D and E one after

another . We have learned that

the interval between the two notes C and E is a third, but its full correct name is a major third. Now play slowly C, D and E *flat*. The mood has changed! You should have felt a cloud blot out your sun! A piece in a minor key often brings to us a sense of seriousness or gravity, though not always. Handel wrote his Dead March from the Oratorio Saul in a major key!

We saw in our example that the D sharp and E flat is the same note on the piano and has the same level of pitch. Indeed, *every* note has an alternative name, depending on whether the music is written in a key using flats or using sharps, and this altering of the letter name of a note without changing its pitch, as with the D sharp to E flat, is known as an **enharmonic** change. And so this particular interval of the augmented second sounds strange and oriental to us, because it appears within the framework of an alien key – again I should like to be able to illustrate this to you in sound, but for instance compare the two following examples and if you yourself cannot find the notes, ask a friend to play it for you!

(a)

(b)

The E flat in example (a) is the same note as D sharp in example (b) but because of the harmony in the bass clef, the treble clef notes in example (b) sound incongruous, conflicting, although somewhat exotic! To sum up then, to the question 'what is an augmented second?', my answer would be 'it is an interval between two notes that are three semitones apart, and which, when heard against certain harmonies, suggest strange, and in particular, oriental associations'.

Now I think I have just about covered the points of musical theory that affect dancers and teachers and indeed choreographers, unless you can think of anything else?

DANCER – Well if we can recap on the subjects we have discussed. You have spoken about musical notation, the values of notes, the construction of scales, time-signatures, simple and compound time, musical terms relating to tempo, expression and dynamics, and lastly intervals. However, I seem to recall your saying earlier that you would elaborate on the uses of the $\frac{3}{4}$ time-signature.

MUSICIAN – Yes, indeed, thank you for reminding me! I said then that $\frac{3}{4}$ time was usually referred to as **waltz-time**. So indeed it is, but what is often forgotten is that both the mazurka and the polonaise are written in $\frac{3}{4}$ and many people do not understand the rhythmic differences between these dances – so let me try to explain!

The graceful waltz, which was the most popular of all dances during the nineteenth century, evolved from its more energetic precursor, the peasant dance known as the Ländler. In a waltz, the accompaniment nearly always consists of a bass note on the first crotchet, with repeated chords on the second and third, thus giving a feeling of a definite accent on the first beat of the bar, e.g. *Sleeping Beauty*.

In a mazurka, the accompaniment is quite often similar to that of a waltz, but this time the accent is more on the second beat of the bar, and sometimes even on the third.

The feeling here is a much livelier one than in the waltz, and even the melody can be considerably accented. Consider these examples:

(a)

The polonaise is a slower dance than the mazurka, but no less marked or accented. Its chief character lies in the rhythm of the accompaniment, which is usually

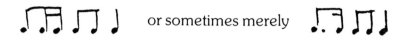 or sometimes merely

When accompanying a class, especially a boys' class, I have frequently been asked to play a slow mazurka, which, with its single beat accompaniment, turned out to be far from inspiring, and without a 'lift', as dancers call it! Quite obviously to me, a polonaise should have been requested, as its fuller and more rhythmic accompaniment provides more drive and impetus to the steps being danced.

DANCER – I find all that very interesting, and it certainly helps to prove that time-signatures in themselves cannot convey speed or indeed any other characteristics of the music.

MUSICIAN – Believe me, a time-signature is only what its name implies – a symbol used by composers when actually writing their music on paper, and which tells the performer, and sometimes the listener or score-reader, how the musical bars are constructed and how many main beats there are in those bars.

DANCER – Could you now please explain briefly about syncopation and cross-rhythms – one hears those terms used so often and I personally find them rather difficult to understand.

MUSICIAN – Yes, indeed – **syncopation** is a word one often comes across, or hears mentioned, and it can set us wondering somewhat! Quite simply, it means that notes or chords are heard, not *on* the main beats of the bar, but between them. Consider for a moment this syncopated melody:

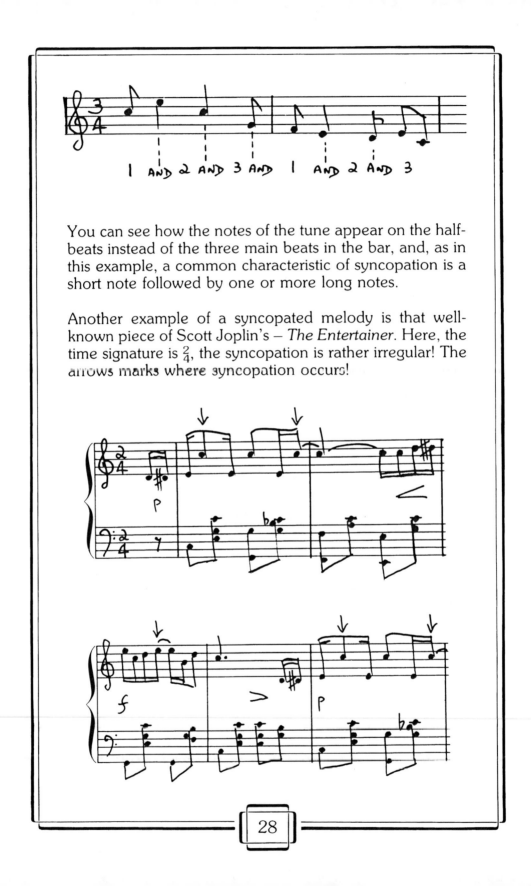

You can see how the notes of the tune appear on the half-beats instead of the three main beats in the bar, and, as in this example, a common characteristic of syncopation is a short note followed by one or more long notes.

Another example of a syncopated melody is that well-known piece of Scott Joplin's – *The Entertainer*. Here, the time signature is $\frac{2}{4}$, the syncopation is rather irregular! The arrows marks where syncopation occurs!

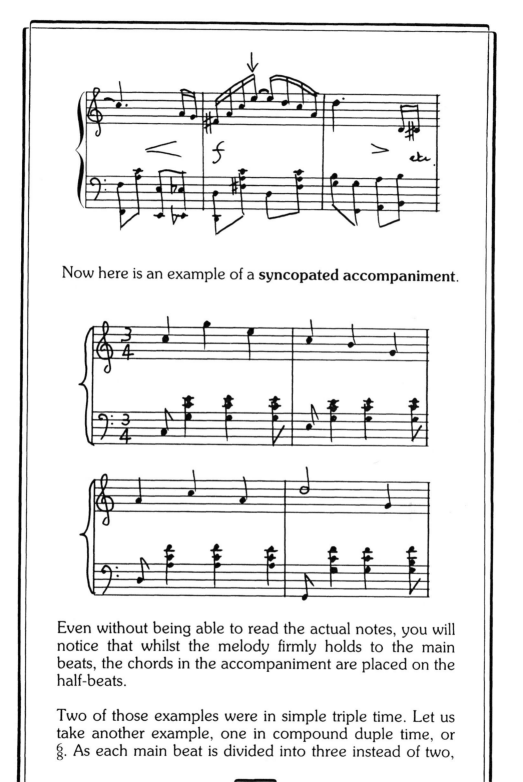

Now here is an example of a **syncopated accompaniment**.

Even without being able to read the actual notes, you will notice that whilst the melody firmly holds to the main beats, the chords in the accompaniment are placed on the half-beats.

Two of those examples were in simple triple time. Let us take another example, one in compound duple time, or $\frac{6}{8}$. As each main beat is divided into three instead of two, any syncopation will have to come on the second or third of each set of triplets. One marvellous instance of this can be seen in that wonderful piece from the *Sleeping Beauty*, called Panorama. Here, Tchaikovsky gives us a flowing melody in what 'sounds' like $\frac{3}{4}$ time, but over a bass line in $\frac{6}{8}$ time! Look at the simple framework of that, without concerning ourselves with the ostinato or continuous chords played by the woodwind.

You can see there how, in each bar, the second and third notes of the melody fall on the third and fifth quavers respectively.

That particular example could also serve as an illustration of a simple **cross-rhythm**, because there are two distinctly different rhythms going on at the same time. To my mind, there is often some confusion over the terms cross-rhythm, cross-accent and cross-phrase. Let me try to elucidate!

Imagine that you are dancing with a partner – you are given a pulse or beat such as $\quad$ = 60 and you are told to dance *three* equal steps within that beat, and your partner is asked to dance *four* equal steps to that same pulse. It could then be said that you are dancing a cross-rhythm to that of your partner, or vice-versa! You may be familiar with a Yugoslav folk dance called Padushka; if so, you will remember that at times you need to dance four steps to the three main beats in the music – you are therefore dancing a cross-rhythm to the music!

A pianist often has to play differing rhythms with each separate hand at the same time. Chopin wrote a study in $\frac{2}{4}$ time where the left hand plays two notes to a beat whilst the right hand plays three. He also wrote a waltz with the usual three-beat oom-pah-pah in the bass, while the actual melody in the right hand consists of *two* main beats! The expression **cross-accent** usually refers to where a regular rhythm is disturbed by shifting the accents. A good example of this can be seen in the Spanish dance, the jota. The dancer performs two bars of regular $\frac{3}{4}$ rhythm 123, 123, but then suddenly, without altering the tempo, dances the next two bars shifting the accents to become **123**, **123**. The normal pattern of accents has been disturbed!

Cross-phrasing is a term mainly used by choreographers of Jazz and Tap dance, and refers to where there is a different number of bars in the musical phrase to that of the sequence of steps. For instance, to eight bars of a $\frac{4}{4}$. Blues, a sequence of steps, i.e. the dancer's phrase, could last for seven crotchets or quarter-notes, be repeated three times, then a one bar 'finish' to coincide with the end of the musician's phrase.

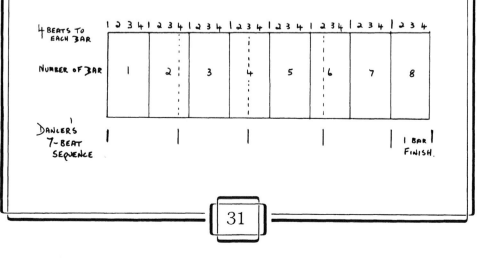

Padushka can be used again for another example of cross-phrasing, because there, the dancer completes two sequences of steps, each of ten bars duration, whilst the musician plays three phrases of eight, four and eight bars.

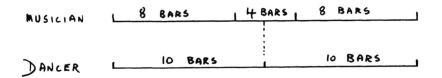

Well, I hope our discussion will have helped to clarify certain musical points, and that you will in future, feel more confident in dealing with musical matters. However, before I finish, I should like to address any of you that are teachers. I have played for many classes in my time, both within and outside the confines of the Royal Ballet, and I should like to make a few observations and suggestions, if I may! Most teachers, I feel, get so set in their own particular routines that they are unwilling to try something new! For example, I know at least one teacher who asks for virtually every exercise to be accompanied by music that is in triple time – waltzes in different speeds and slow $\frac{3}{4}$ music for adage. Now this becomes exceedingly boring and irritating, both for the wretched pianist who is trying to please the teacher, and also of course for the pupils. Many times I have suggested that, for example, in the adage section, music in a slow $\frac{4}{4}$ time or a $\frac{12}{8}$ should be used. There are so many wonderful tunes in those time-signatures that it is very regrettable that they should be excluded from class by a stubborn teacher.

In my own books of pieces, both original and arranged, published by the Imperial Society, I went to great pains to include music for adage in quadruple time, and $\frac{12}{8}$ particularly can convey a wonderfully smooth and flowing impression of movement. All that a sceptical or wavering teacher needs to do is to ask for a short session alone with a pianist and if necessary, to make a tape of suitable music, so that he or she can prepare enchainements and get used to working in that particular rhythm. Who knows, it might not be long before they actually request an adage in quadruple time! One particular male teacher used to delight in asking me to play something with eleven beats to the phrase! This is not too difficult for a pianist who is proficient in improvising, but it just goes to show that he had taken the trouble to work out a particular exercise in an unusual timing to allay monotony in class, and if someone can do that with elevens, how much easier it should be to try using fours!

Now I should like to say something about counting! It is of course, a very good way of learning the length of phrases in music, both for dancers and musicians. I often count to myself when there are a number of bars of repetitive music, especially at the end of certain pieces (Tchaikovsky was very fond of writing such passages at the end of variations!). Instead of keeping my eyes glued to the score, I memorise the number of bars, so that I can focus my attention on the dancer! In a difficult ballet such as *The Rite of Spring*, it is virtually the only way a dancer can understand the complicated and uneven rhythms in Stravinsky's score, but I must confess that I rather resent being able to *hear* the dancers counting during a performance! The only disadvantage of counting is that it sometimes bears no relation to the way the music is written down.

For example, I was somewhat worried when I heard a teacher, instructing a young pupil in the polka, count the rhythm of the steps as – 'and one, two, three – and one, two, three'. Little wonder that when the child was asked in an exam what time-signature a polka was usually written in, she replied $\frac{3}{4}$! Try to count always in relation to the musical notation – in this case, 'and one and two', or

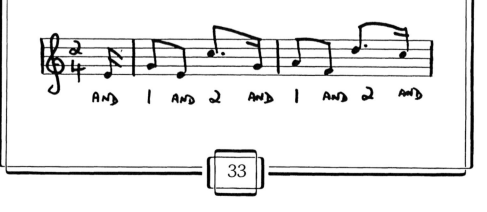

Quite often, when you are doing choreography, you will want to use a piece of music that is too long and which will need to be shortened or 'cut' as we say. Now, this is no job for anyone who cannot read music! There are so many factors which have to be taken into account, amongst them being form and key. Every piece of music is written in some pattern or other, (this of course, is a subject in itself!) and this form or shape *must* be considered when reducing the length of the piece. Similarly, the cutting must be done in such a way as to obviate any sudden and noticeably disturbing change of key! This task should always be done by a competent musician, so don't take chances – ask!

Finally, if the ideas in this little book have stimulated in you a real interest in music, and you have a desire to be considered a more musical dancer than the next person, do learn as much as you can about it! You do not necessarily have to play an instrument – there are many books that can help you to *listen* properly, and that can advance your understanding of musical theory. It is impossible to know too much! So get working – and good luck!